The boy wl cried wolf

Story written by Alison Hawes
Illustrated by Tim Archbold

Speed Sounds

Consonants   *Ask children to say the sounds.*

f	l	m	n	r	s	v	z	sh	th	ng
ff	ll	mm	nn	rr	ss	ve	zz			nk
ph	le	mb	kn	wr	se		(**se**)			
			gn		(**c**)		s			
					ce					

b	c	d	g	h	j	p	qu	t	w	x	y	ch
bb	k	dd	g		g	pp		tt	(**wh**)			tch
	ck		gg		ge							
			gu		dge							

Each box contains one sound but sometimes more than one grapheme.
*Focus graphemes for this story are **circled**.*

4

Vowels

Ask children to say the sounds in and out of order.

a	e ea	i	o	u	ay a͡-e a	(ee) (ea) (y) (e)	igh i͡-e ie i	ow o͡-e o oe
at	hen	in	on	up	day	see	high	blow

oo u͡-e ue	oo	ar	or oor ore aw	air are	ir ur er	ou ow	oy oi
zoo	look	car	for	fair	whirl	shout	boy

Story Green Words

Ask children to read the words first in Fred Talk and then say the word.

flock   noise   each   safe   wolf*   lie*   cried*

Ask children to say the syllables and then read the whole word.

Iss|am   hun|gry   vill|age   a|sleep   sulk|i|ly   nev|er*

Ask children to read the root first and then the whole word with the suffix.

live → lived   dream → dreaming   sudden → suddenly

trick → tricks   attack → attacking   trust → trusted

place → places   plea → pleas   ignore → ignored

* Challenge Words

6

Vocabulary Check

Discuss the meaning (as used in the story) after the children have read each word.

	definition:	sentence:
live up to	be as good as	"We trust you to live up to your name," said his mother.
flock	a group of sheep	Each day, Issam took the flock of sheep up to the hills…
dull	boring	Keeping the sheep safe was important, but Issam found it dull.
pleas	calls	But the people ignored his pleas for help.
wept	cried	"The flock is lost," he wept.

Red Words

all	once	where	could
other	some	would	who
people	were	mother	over
why	now	through	what
there	any	one	old

The boy who cried wolf

Issam had an important job. He needed to keep all the sheep safe from the hungry wolf that lived in the hills.

"We trust you to live up to your name," said his mother. She never let him forget that his name meant 'to keep safe'.

Each day, Issam took the flock of sheep up into the hills to eat the sweet, green grass.

Keeping the sheep safe was important, but Issam found it dull.
He lay in the grass dreaming of all the places he wished he could be.
He wanted to have some *fun*!

One day, Issam was so bored
he did something shocking.
He stood at the top of the
hill and cried out:

"Wolf! Wolf! A wolf is
attacking the sheep!
I need your help!"

The people from the village rushed up the hill
to help Issam keep the flock safe. But when they
reached him, there was no wolf to be seen.

"Issam – where is the wolf?" they shouted.

"There isn't one!" he mumbled.

"We trusted you," they cried. "What will your mother say?"

"Can't a boy have a bit of fun?" Issam said, sulkily.

The very next day he did the same thing.

"Wolf! Wolf!" he cried. "Please be quick or the wolf will eat the sheep!"

The people from the village rushed up the hill but, as before, there was no wolf. You have never seen people so angry! They shouted. They screamed. They yelled.

"No more tricks! We cannot trust you if you keep doing this."

The next day, Issam was asleep beneath
a leafy tree. Suddenly, the air was filled
with the noise of bleating sheep.

Issam leapt to his feet.
"Oh no!" he screamed.
"It's a wolf!"

"Wolf! Wolf!" he cried, as loudly as he could.

But the people ignored his pleas for help.
"It's just one of Issam's tricks," they told each other.

"Help!" cried Issam. "There really *is* a wolf."
But nobody came. Nobody helped.
The wolf killed all the sheep.

Issam dragged his feet back to the village.
"The flock is lost," he wept. "Why didn't you help me?"

The people were very angry.
"You really do not know?" they shouted.
"Why do you think? We could not
trust you. And now you have lost
all our sheep."

Issam looked at the ground, red-faced.
From then on, he never told a lie.
But he became known as 'the boy who cried wolf'.

Questions to talk about

Ask children to TTYP each question using 'Fastest finger' (FF) or 'Have a think' (HaT).

p.9 (FF) What was Issam's job?

p.10 (HaT) Why did Issam pretend there was a wolf attacking the sheep?

p.11 (FF) Why did the people rush up the hill?

p.12 (HaT) Why were the people from the village so angry?

p.14 (HaT) Why do you think the people ignored Issam?

p.15 (HaT) Issam said, "The flock is lost." What does this mean?

p.15 (HaT) Issam looked at the ground, red-faced. What does this tell you about how he felt?

Questions to read and answer

(Children complete without your help.)

1. Issam's name meant **to keep well / to keep healthy / to keep safe**.

2. Issam was **happy / bored / shocked** watching the sheep.

3. "A wolf is attacking the sheep!" cried **Issam's mother / the people / Issam**.

4. The people said they could not **trust / see / reach** Issam.

5. From then on, Issam never told a **tale / story / lie**.

Speedy Green Words

Ask children to practise reading the words across the rows, down the columns and in and out of order clearly and quickly.

help	need	name	say
day	angry	eat	sweet
really	hills	seen	boy
sheep	air	next	feet
our	live	tree	please

Phonics

The boy who cried wolf

OXFORD
UNIVERSITY PRESS

How to get in touch:

web   www.oxfordprimary.co.uk
email primary.enquiries@oup.com
tel.   +44 (0) 1536 452610
fax   +44 (0) 1865 313472

ISBN 978-1-382-01350-5

9 781382 013505

A Guide to Bodmin Jail
and its History

Bill Johnson